UX TO GO

A handy, quick-start guide
for wannabe designers

Lorraine Phillips

Author: Lorraine Phillips
Editor: Marilyn Burkley

Cover and interior design: Lorraine Phillips
Website: uxtogo.net

ISBN-13: 978-0-9889535-8-1
ISBN-10: 0-9889535-8-7
LCCN: 2022917042

Library of Congress subject headings:
1. User interfaces (Computer systems).
2. Design.

Published by:
360 Books LLC
PO Box 361721
Atlanta, GA 30036
www.3sixtybooks.com

First Printing
Printed in the United States of America

Acknowledgments

Thanks to Martin Van de Loo, who first introduced me to UX in a chance encounter many years ago. I also have to give an honorable mention to my partner in crime back then, by the name of Deniss Bohanovs.

Thanks to Justina Ampofo and Annetta LaCroix (my UX counsel) for just being you.

Thanks to Paul Capcan for kindly granting me permission to use a couple of the assets found at uxhints.com.

Thanks to Josette Jeffers and Jamoi for my author pic.

And lastly, a special thanks goes out to my family and all those who have helped me in *any way*, along the way—you know who you are because you hear it daily.

Table of Contents

Introduction

What you have here is basically the contents of my notebook. It's most of what I've seen, heard, experienced, studied, learned, read, or created along my journey in UX.

It's definitely not the be-all and end-all, but I'm hoping at the very least it will be a good start. I wanted to create something you could read in a couple of sittings but come back to reference time and time again. I chose to go wide (and even that's somewhat limited) rather than deep, but the idea is to give you enough information that you can choose to go deeper with on your own.

The field is so varied and pulls from so many disciplines that there's no way anyone could possibly write about it all; plus, UX is a constantly moving target. But that's what makes it fun, challenging, and exciting–it forces you to become a lifelong learner, which fits perfectly well with me.

I truly enjoy the field of UX (in case you couldn't tell, I wrote a short guide about it) and I'm hoping you come to enjoy it just as much too. Keep me posted–let me know how it all works out.

Lorraine Phillips

Chapter 1:
The Goal of UX Design

The goal of UX (user experience) design is to make technology easier and more enjoyable to use, so people can do what they want or need to do without difficulty or frustration. There are several factors that affect the overall experience a user has with a product, as we'll explore here by taking a look at some of the causes and characteristics of both good and not-so-good UX design.

Good UX Design

Good UX design...

- Solves a problem
- Is useful (in that it fulfills a need)
- Is simple and intuitive
- Demands as little effort from the user as possible (mental or otherwise)
- Doesn't get in the way of the user (good design is ultimately invisible)
- Provides a consistent functional and visual experience throughout (which plays a key part in the learnability of a product)

- Is responsive, which means the content, layout, and functionality adapt to—and are optimized for—the size and type of screen or device being used
- Is accessible, in that it accommodates the needs of people with diverse abilities, including vision, hearing, motor, and cognitive impairments
- Is equitable, in that it takes into account the needs of people from diverse backgrounds who have traditionally been underrepresented in the past (think along the lines of race, gender, class, religion, sexual identity, sexual orientation, and nationality)
- Matches a user's mental model. It is important to consider the experiences and interactions users have had in the past that may influence the way they use a product now. It's easier for a user to understand new concepts if they are largely based on what they already know or are familiar with; therefore, it's important to aim to match your design to the way a user currently thinks—unless, of course, it makes absolute sense not to.
- Is visually appealing
- Is logically organized (this includes navigation)
- Is free of unnecessary interruptions or distractions (think self-serving pop-ups and ads)
- Helps along the way by providing contextual suggestions and cues
- Makes mistakes easy to avoid or recover from
- Gives feedback that lets a user feel in control, answering questions like: What's happening? What just happened? What's about to happen? Where am I? Where did I just come from? Where can I go next? What can I do now?
- Uses simple, familiar terms (avoids jargon)

- Features content that is easy to scan
- Uses conversational microcopy (microcopy is the snippets of text that help a user take an action, often appearing as error messages, captions, or button text, etc.)
- Is engaging
- Is efficient
- Is effective
- Provides a seamless experience across devices. For instance, if I put an item in my shopping cart on Amazon while on my phone, I expect to be able to pick up where I left off when I log in later on my laptop. (It is estimated that 90 percent of multiple-device owners switch between screens to complete tasks, using an average of three different combinations each day.)
- Has a limited set of features (think quality over quantity)
- Follows the 80/20 rule, better known as the Pareto principle. This rule, when applied to products, means that 80 percent of a product's benefit comes from just 20 percent of its features. Make the most useful 20 percent of your feature set easy to discover by cleverly hiding the other 80 percent.

Not-So-Good UX Design

Not-so-good UX design can be...

- Frustrating
- Confusing
- Difficult
- Cumbersome
- Unintuitive
- Complicated
- Time-consuming

What causes it:

- Not truly understanding a user's problem or need
- Conducting an insufficient amount of market and user research
- Not validating designs with actual users (no usability testing performed)
- Feature bloat, resulting in an overly complex product that no longer addresses core user needs
- Lack of structure, organization, logical flow, or visual hierarchy (where elements are arranged according to importance)
- Tasks and features not prioritized and displayed according to importance
- Inconsistent app behavior (not predictable or reliable, making the product hard to learn)
- Non-descriptive, unintuitive labeling
- Information overload (providing too much information or being too wordy throughout)
- A lack of customer support or contextual help
- Carrying out design just for the sake of design, while completely ignoring the words or content that support it. Aim for a content-driven approach (which means absolutely no lorem ipsum ever, please). As I once read, "design without text is decoration." Ouch!
- Developing innovative ideas for the sake of innovation, rather than relying on familiar patterns or mental models
- Not understanding that UX is about problem solving and not about art or self-expression
- Creating fancy animated UIs that are not easy to use
- The ineffective use of white space, resulting in a cluttered, cramped, difficult-to-use interface
- Not engaging developers early enough in the process

Chapter 2:
The Many Flavors of UX

If one thing is certain, it's that none of the following roles, titles, or duties are written in stone anywhere—on the face of this planet, anyway. If you're not somewhat comfortable with change and ambiguity, then I'd go so far as to say that UX might not be the right field for you.

Responsibilities will vary according to the industry, size, and maturity level of the company you work for—as well as your personal level of experience. You can expect there to be overlap; a designer may carry out research or even do a little UX writing, and a UX writer may be involved in UI design. The main thing is to just remain as flexible as possible. Stay inquisitive and ready to learn, and, of course, carry out your job to the best of your ability—because at the end of the day that's all that really matters anyway.

Product development is a team effort and, ideally, you'll be working in a multidisciplinary, cross-functional team that may include project managers, content designers, UX writers, researchers, engineers, quality assurance (QA), marketing, sales, and whomever else you may need to collaborate with in solving your customers' problems or needs.

Focusing more on the UX side of the house, here's a list of the professionals (along with their duties) you're most likely to collaborate with.

UX Designer / Product Designer

A UX designer builds simple, intuitive, engaging experiences that enable users to easily accomplish their tasks and goals. They work on websites, apps, or other digital products, developing new products and services from scratch or making enhancements to existing ones. A UX designer is also responsible for making sure a product or service meets the needs of the business–developing solutions that completely align with a business's vision, strategy, and goals.

Tools used by UX designers include Figma, FigJam, Sketch, InVision Studio, Flinto, Framer, Marvel, Proto.io, Axure RP, UXPin, and Balsamiq.

User Interface (UI) Designer

UI designers create the look and feel of an application's interface. As experts in color theory, typography, imagery, and iconography, they use their expert knowledge to make designs visually and emotionally appealing to the target audience. Check out sites like Dribbble or Behance for amazing examples of UI design. It's not until you drop those visuals into some type of flow that you'll actually be able to evaluate the user experience, however, so don't be intimidated in the least…be inspired.

Tools used by UI designers include Figma, FigJam, Sketch, InVision Studio, Flinto, Framer, Marvel, Proto.io, Axure RP, UXPin, Balsamiq, Photoshop, and Illustrator.

Information Architect (IA) / UX Architect

The aim of an information architect is to increase the usability of a product by structuring, organizing, and labeling content in a clear and logical manner so the information a user needs is easy to find, discover, navigate, scan, or read. While the "information architect" title is often reserved for larger, more mature organizations, this very important discipline now more commonly falls under the realm of either UX or content design.

Tools used by information architects include Figma, FigJam, Sketch, InVision Studio, Axure RP, Microsoft Visio, DYNO Mapper, Screaming Frog, SmartDraw, Whimsical, and Zen Flowchart.

UX Writer

A UX writer creates the clear, concise, sometimes conversational interface copy (microcopy) that helps a user understand, use, and navigate a product. Their words appear on buttons, labels, captions, icons, forms, contextual help and tooltips, error messages, pop-ups, and more.

To ensure that language remains consistent regardless of who (or what department) creates the content, a UX writer needs to become familiar with a company's content style guide (if indeed they have one). A content style guide is a company-wide document that outlines a particular brand's rules for creating content. This includes the voice (personality), tone (mood), style, vocabulary, grammar, and other specifics that should be adhered to for the purpose of creating content. You can find excellent examples of content style guides online from Intuit, Mailchimp, Atlassian, and Shopify–just to name a few.

Tools used by UX writers include Google Docs, Mural, Miro, Figma, FigJam, Sketch, Ditto (a plugin made for Figma), and Frontitude (a plugin that primarily works with Figma and Sketch).

Content Designer

The content designer's role is similar to that of a UX writer but takes on a much broader perspective: planning, writing, editing, and managing content that is informed by research and an understanding of the holistic user journey, to help in the design of websites, apps, and other digital products.

Tools used by content designers include Google Docs, Miro, Mural, Figma, FigJam, Sketch, Ditto (a plugin made for Figma), and Frontitude (a plugin that primarily works with Figma and Sketch).

Content Strategist

The content strategist's role is similar to that of a content designer, except that they take a more high-level, strategic approach to planning, creating, publishing, and managing content to achieve a specific business or user goal. It is ultimately the art of bringing the right content to the right person at the right time in a way that helps to maximize the usability and profitability of the content. This content can consist of absolutely anything that is used to convey meaningful information, including text, photos, graphics, illustrations, graphs, charts, diagrams, infographics, and video.

You may find a content strategist performing content audits (a quantitative and qualitative assessment of all content that lives online); maintaining style guides, editorial calendars, or taxonomies (the term used to describe, organize, and classify content); or overseeing content migration plans where content is moved from one content management system (CMS) to another.

UX Researcher

UX researchers are responsible for providing insights into user wants, needs, goals, motivations, attitudes, expectations, and pain points so an organization can move from opinion-driven design to a more informed, empathetic, customer-focused, and data-driven design.

UX researchers collect and analyze data using both quantitative and qualitative methods. Quantitative research focuses on behaviors that can be measured and expressed in numbers or figures. For instance, how many users signed up for a service or made a purchase, or how long did it take for a user to complete a task and how many errors did they encounter along the way? The method works best when you have something to compare to, whether it be a previous design, a competitor, or an industry standard. In the absence of comparison data, a baseline should be established, and measurements can be taken from there.

Qualitative research, on the other hand, emphasizes non-numerical insights, focusing more on thoughts, feelings, emotions, opinions, and experiences—answering the "what," "how," and "why" of a user's behavior rather than "how many" or "how much."

Quantitative research methods:
- A/B testing
- Multivariate testing
- Analytic reporting
- Card sorting
- Eye-tracking studies
- Surveys and questionnaires that ask closed-ended questions and have a limited set of options to respond to
- Tree testing (unmoderated)

Qualitative research methods:
- Diary studies
- Field studies
- Focus groups
- Surveys and questionnaires that ask open-ended questions
- Tree testing (moderated)
- User interviews
- Usability testing

Tools used by UX researchers include Hotjar, Lookback, Loop11, Maze, Optimal Workshop, Optimizely, Survey-Monkey, Typeform, UserTesting, Userlytics, UserZoom, and UsabilityHub.

Chapter 3:
Common UX Docs and Deliverables

This chapter will introduce some of the documents and deliverables you're most likely to encounter in your role as a UX designer. Definitely not an exhaustive list (if you can believe that), the following docs will help team members extract, synthesize, and communicate findings in somewhat of a presentable, standardized format. Presenting findings in this way makes it easier to receive feedback from stakeholders and get teams aligned around the problem space as a whole.

Affinity Diagram / Affinity Map

An affinity diagram allows you to organize and categorize ideas, concepts, or information into groups of similar items by identifying patterns or themes that exist between them. If you've ever seen a group of people standing around a whiteboard of some sort with stickies and markers in hand, then you were more than likely witnessing an affinity diagramming exercise in progress.

Figure 1: Affinity diagramming exercise

Affinity mapping tools include FigJam, InVision Freehand, Miro, Mural, Microsoft Visio, Lucidchart, and, of course, Post-it Notes and pens.

Card Sorting

In UX research, card sorting is used to organize, categorize, and label information based on the feedback received from a selected audience. Participants from the audience are asked to organize items into the groups or categories that make the most sense to them. Card sorting is commonly used to create intuitive, user-friendly navigation systems and interfaces.

Card sorts can be one of the following:
- Open, where participants create the labels for the groups they choose themselves
- Closed, where participants are asked to place items into preset categories (see figure 2)

- Hybrid, where categories are predefined (as in a closed card sort) but participants are free to create their own categories as well, outside of what's already been provided

The activity can be moderated, allowing for more qualitative insight into particular selections, or unmoderated, where a facilitator is not required. To be able to detect significant patterns in results, it is advised that between 30 and 60 cards be used, along with 20 to 30 participants.

Figure 2: Closed card sort example for a university site

Application Process	Academic Experience	Student Life	About	
Campus Highlights	Our Faculty	Deadlines and Forms	News and Events	International Applicants
University Policies	Living on Campus	Virtual Tour	Departments and Programs	Mission and History
Military Applicants	Financial Aid	Undergraduate Admissions	Campus Bookstore	Clubs and Organizations
Fees and Tuition	Housing and Dining	Diversity and Inclusion	Graduate Admissions	Scholarships

Card-sorting tool: Optimal Workshop (highly recommended).

Competitive Analysis

Competitive analysis should be carried out as early in the UX design process as possible. It'll be impossible to build a great product if you completely ignore the competition–and with so much to learn from them, there really is no need for you to reinvent the wheel.

Analyze the overall end-to-end experience of your top three to five competitors, looking at the flow, features, functionality, patterns, and UI. How is information presented and organized? What do they do well and what could be improved? Which tasks are prominently featured? What's somewhat hidden and less accessible? Why do you think that is? What similarities do they share and in what ways do they differ from each other? What customer pain points are they failing to address? What could be removed (or simplified) to allow for a more streamlined approach? The wealth of information you'll gather from carrying out this exercise will help you identify strategic opportunities that can be used to develop a solution that has the ability to launch with a significant competitive edge.

Social media chat rooms and discussion boards are another great source of information–your competitors' customers are out there and they're talking. It may also be worth checking into similar products that may have failed in the past in an attempt to determine some of the reasons behind their failure.

To document and share your findings, use whatever format you find to be most effective–a deck, a spreadsheet, or a combination of any of the other types of deliverables you find in this chapter.

Customer Journey Map (See Figure 3)

A customer journey map visualizes the linear path a customer (or persona) takes to engage with a particular product or service being offered by a business. In addition to showing the interactions that take place along the way, the map provides insight into what a customer is doing, thinking, and feeling at every stage of the process.

Visualizing the journey in this way allows us to understand key pain points, identify business opportunities, and assign responsibility for friction-causing touchpoints to the relevant teams or departments (whether sales, marketing, customer service, SEO, or UX, etc.) so they can do their part in optimizing a customer's overall experience.

Empathy Map (See Figure 4)

An empathy map is used to gain a better understanding of a user by helping us identify what it feels like to be them. Compiled from qualitative user research data, an empathy map presents a user (or persona) at the center of the diagram surrounded by four quadrants that describe what they said, did, thought, and felt.

Experience Map

An experience map focuses on the end-to-end journey (or path) a customer takes to purchase a product or service. It differs from a customer journey map in that it is not tied to a specific user, product, service, or business. Organizations use this high-level approach to establish a baseline for general human behavior in achieving a specific goal before even taking a particular product or service into consideration.

Figure 3: Customer journey map example (Used with permission from Paul Capcan of uxhints.com)

STAGES	Awareness	Consideration	Acquisition	Service	Loyalty
STEPS	Wants to find a TV provider	Needs to choose a provider	Subscribes to a plan	Uses the service	Extends service subscription
THINKING	- Who's on the market?	- Who is the best provider? - What are the prices? - What do people prefer? - What are the features?	- Is there a discount? - Is there a trial? - How to pay? - How to cancel the membership?	- How good is the quality? - How good is support? - How to connect a new device?	- Is there going to be more content? - Is there going to be new features? - Will the price change?
DOING		Wants to start researching	- Goes to the website - Searches the web for feedback - Compares prices - Compares features	- Makes decision - Pays for subscription - Starts trial - Installs the equipment/software	- Uses the service - Builds playlists, favourites, bookmarks - Connects new devices	- Extends subscription - Recommends the service - Joins the community (forum, slack channels, etc)
FEELING	🙂	😕	😐	😟	😀
PAIN POINTS	- Is not aware of all products - Doesn't know what to choose - Doubts the value of the product	- Doesn't know where to start - Doesn't want to spend a lot of time on research	- Can't pay by BitCoin - The payment process is unclear	- Hard to build playlists - Hard to find content - Not enough content - Buffering issues	- No discounts - Not enough other incentives
OPPORTUNITIES	- Empower word of mouth - Extend marketing channels	- Create positive image of the product - Contextual promo - Decrease frictions for trial opportunities	- Improve payment UX - Support more payments systems	- Improve playlists UX - Provide better streaming quality - Increase content discoverability	- Create loyalty programs - Turn users into advocates - Offer partner programms - Improve discounts model

Figure 4: Empathy map template (Used with permission from Paul Capcan)

Flowchart / Flow Diagram (See Figure 5)

A flowchart is usually synthesized early in the design process (following the initial user research). It is an extremely high-level, bare-bones representation of the steps a user can take through a system to accomplish a goal. It is best to keep the charts clean and simple by showing one path at a time, with other flows being developed to demonstrate what happens when the user wishes to accomplish a different goal.

Symbols used for the diagram include the following:
- Ovals to signify entry and exit points
- Rectangles to indicate a process or action step
- Diamonds to show decision points
- Arrows that show the direction a user takes based on the decisions made

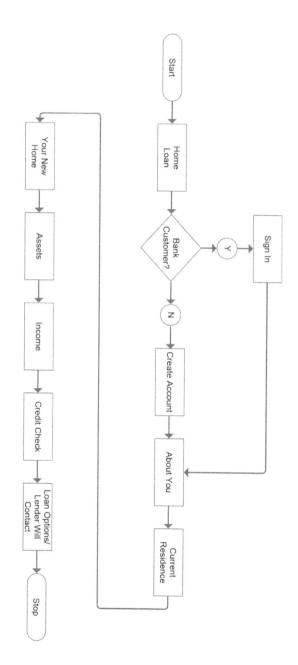

Figure 5: Flowchart for an example mortgage application flow

Flowcharting tools include Figma, Axure RP, Lucidchart, Microsoft Visio, SmartDraw, Whimsical, and Zen Flowchart.

Interactive Prototype

Your most important deliverable as a UX designer will be an interactive prototype, which allows you to bring your ideas to life without committing the time, money, and resources necessary for building the actual product. An interactive prototype can range in fidelity from low to high, and as a sample version of the final product, includes basic interactions, transitions, and events that can be used to demonstrate functionality to stakeholders, tease feedback from team members, and help validate concepts with potential users. You'll have to use your imagination here as far as the interactivity and movement from screen to screen... but you get the picture.

Figure 6: High-fidelity interactive prototype example

Interactive prototyping tools include Figma, Sketch, InVision Studio, Flinto, Framer, Marvel, Proto.io, Axure RP, and UXPin.

Persona (See Figure 7)

A persona is a fictional character (composed from the results of qualitative and quantitative user research) that is used to classify and summarize the characteristics of the most important users a product will serve. It is common to have up to four personas for a project, with one (or possibly two) serving as the primary persona that the majority of features must satisfy—and all others serving as secondary.

The tool not only helps to get a business aligned around exactly who it's designing for, but also aids in understanding, relating to, and remembering the user throughout the entire design process. If this is done well, your team will eventually start referring to these personas as if they were real people, and that's the whole idea.

Information listed for a persona can include the following:
- A believable photo of the user
- A memorable, relatable name
- A short bio
- A quote that summarizes what matters most in regard to your product
- Age
- Gender
- Ethnicity
- Family status
- Domicile (city or country)
- Level of education
- Occupation

Figure 7: Persona example

Julie Roberts

Human Resources Manager

> I'm a breast cancer survivor who has been advised by my doctor to cut back on all meats and incorporate more veggies into my diet. Becoming pescatarian will allow me to do that.

Bio

Age: 48
Marital Status: Married
Dependents: 2
Education: Master's degree
Tech Level: Advanced

Goals

· Adopt a healthy lifestyle
· Give up meat
· Incorporate more fruits and vegetables into her diet
· Limit the amount of dairy
· Continue to cook for her family without too much disruption

Needs

· App that makes learning about meatless foods, substitutes, recipes and snacks simple and easy
· Meals that ensure she is getting the recommended daily amounts of vitamins and nutrients
· Recipes that allow her to align what she cooks for her family with the equivalent meatless (or pescatarian) version for herself
· The ability to create shopping lists that conveniently have specific products and brands listed, so she does not have to take the time to read food labels at the store

Frustrations

· Unsure where to start with becoming pescatarian
· Not sure how to maintain a healthy diet without meat
· Cannot find specific info with dietary concerns around the subject
· Apps are geared toward vegetarians and vegans (nothing specifically for pescatarians)
· Does not want to disrupt her family's lifestyle even though her diet is changing

- Title
- Salary
- A brief description of their family life and motivations
- Hobbies
- Tech level (beginner, intermediate, or advanced)
- Context of use of the product (the "where")
- The "why" behind their use of the product
- Pain points, problems, or frustrations
- Goals or needs

Sitemap

The sitemap is a visual tool for planning and organizing the navigational structure, content, and labeling of the major categories and subcategories of a website or app.

Figure 8: Sitemap example

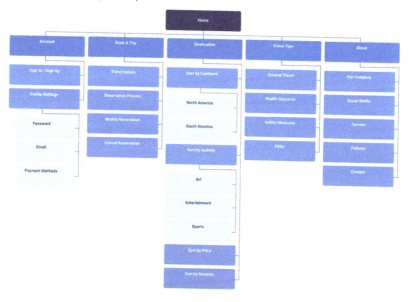

Storyboard (See Figure 9)

A storyboard is a cartoon-like illustration that explains a user problem–depicting the situation that sets it in motion, the thoughts and feelings a user experiences along the way, and the series of actions that must be taken for the issue to be resolved. Originally created by Walt Disney Studios in the 1930s, storyboards were used to visualize the plot of a movie by drawing the different scenes onto pieces of paper and pinning each of them in sequence to a bulletin board.

Don't feel like you need a degree in fine arts to use this technique–quick and dirty works best. As you will see from figure 9, there's absolutely no shame in my game. Just use stick figures, star men, or whatever else you can think of to communicate your ideas.

Task Analysis

Task analysis is the process of capturing the sequence of steps a user must take to achieve a goal so you're able to build a system that supports them in achieving that goal. Knowing that every goal has a beginning and an end point (the desired outcome), your objective is to figure out the intermediary steps (or subtasks) that take place between them–also taking into consideration the effect the physical environment may have on the process. Once you have steps listed, it's important to identify what can be eliminated, optimized, or automated to make the system as convenient and user-friendly as possible.

Goal: User wants to refill liquid soap or shampoo at the nearest self-service dispensary kiosk

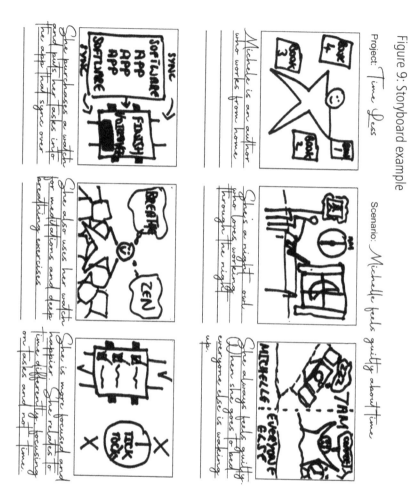

Figure 9: Storyboard example

Steps:
1. User downloads and registers in-app
2. User searches in app for nearest refill station
3. User drives to nearest refill station
4. User scans QR code from app
5. User confirms payment method to use
6. Slot opens and user puts appropriately sized container in slot (sensor automatically detects size)
7. User selects "Soap" or "Shampoo"

8. User selects the desired brand from the list
9. Cost savings are displayed on-screen and user accepts the dollar amount charge for the transaction
10. Liquid is dispensed
11. Kiosk asks: "Fill Another?"
12. User selects "No"
13. Payment is charged, user receives text receipt, and transaction details are registered to the app

Quick tip: This is a design challenge that can be found online. For more context around this problem, see the appendix on page 83.

User Flow

A user flow is a visual representation of the paths a user can take to complete certain tasks within a system. Providing a little more detail than a simple flowchart, it is more UI focused, combining screens at various levels of fidelity depending on how far you are in the process.

Figure 10: User flow example

Usability Test

Usability tests allow you to validate designs by getting your wireframes or prototypes out in front of real users. Having used some (if not most) of the tools presented in this chapter, it's time to get some solid feedback on how useful and usable your designs actually are and find out whether they satisfy user needs–because, after all, this is supposed to be for *them*, right?

You'll need to create a test plan that includes a list of tasks depicting the most common scenarios a user will encounter while using your product based on the goals they'll wish to achieve. To gain extra insight, instruct participants to provide a running commentary of their thoughts as they complete each task (dubbed the "think-aloud method") while you record, watch, listen, and take notes on any usability problems that may arise.

Usability testing is not a one-and-done activity; you'll be testing repeatedly from early development right until release and beyond, iteratively making updates and improvements based on the feedback or metrics you receive. Here are some metrics you may want to consider:

Directness: The number of users who completed a task without hesitation and arrived at the correct answer or destination on their first try.

Success rate: The percentage of users who successfully completed a task.

Error rate: The percentage of users who made a mistake or took a wrong path during a task. (Note that errors and usability problems are inextricably linked.)

Time on task: The time it took a user to complete a task. Although not a super-reliable metric (due to the number of distractions a user may have in the real world) this metric is still worth taking note of.

Effort: The number of clicks, swipes, gestures, etc., necessary to complete a task.

Number of confusions: The number of times a user looked confused, lost, or frustrated.

Level of confidence in selections: This can be measured by attaching a five-point Likert scale at the end of each task with values that range from "Not confident at all" to "Very confident."

Once all tasks are complete, gather feedback on a user's *overall* experience, considering the following:

Usability: To capture overall usability, ask users how they would rate the product on a five-point Likert scale with values ranging from "Extremely easy to use" to "Extremely difficult."

Satisfaction: To evaluate the level of satisfaction, use a five-point Likert scale with values ranging from "Very satisfied" to "Very dissatisfied," with a neutral option in the middle that reads "Neither satisfied nor dissatisfied."

Dislikes: Find out if there's anything the user dislikes about your product. Never open this can of worms by asking the question outright; instead, ask, "If you could change one thing about this product, what would it be?"

User Stories

In the agile software development process (as will be discussed in the upcoming chapter), user stories capture the requirements for a system from a user's perspective in a short, simple, nontechnical way. Stories can be written by the product owner, product manager, dev team, or other contributing team member. They help all involved stay focused on the user and the desired outcome, as opposed to zoning in on a specific solution or feature way too early in the process. It is only after defining the end goal of a story that a team should start ideating around a possible solution. User stories capture the "who," "what," and "why" of a requirement using the following format:

As a <type of user>, **I want to** <achieve a goal>, **so I** <list the benefit>.

Examples include:
- As a business traveler, I want to see hotels that have a business center, so I can access business equipment and services for free.
- As a buyer, I want to securely store my credit card information online, so I don't have to type in my number every time I make a purchase.
- As a learner, I want to see transcripts of the instructional videos, so I can easily copy and paste straight into my notes.

Wireframe (See Figure 11)

In much the same way as an architect creates a blueprint to plan for the construction of a home, wireframes are used to communicate initial ideas for the basic layout and structure of a website, app, or other digital product. The wireframe's skeletal approach provides an overview of where UI elements (such as text blocks, images, buttons, links, navigation, search, etc.) are expected to appear–with all styling, color, and imagery kept to the bare minimum. This lack of attention to the visual design means that team members can zero in and focus on the core functionality of a user's experience, as opposed to getting all caught up in the aesthetics of the design. The tool encourages collaboration, communication, and feedback early in the design process and can range in fidelity from low to high.

Figure 11: Low-fidelity wireframe example

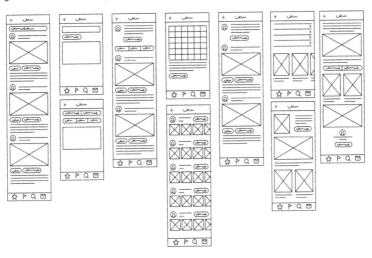

Wireframing tools include Figma, FigJam, Sketch, InVision Studio, and Balsamiq (which is my personal favorite for this purpose).

Chapter 4:
Design Processes

Design Thinking

Design thinking is an iterative, nonlinear, user-centric approach to the practical resolution of customer problems (see figure 12). Although the actual process may vary according to the company or product in question, the overall ethos will tend to remain the same.

Empathize

The first stage of this user-centered design process allows you to set aside your own biases, assumptions, and viewpoints by gaining real-world insight into your users and their problems–conducting interviews, surveys, and observation sessions that help you to gain deep understanding on a psychological and emotional level so you can develop products that make their lives easier and satisfy their needs.

Define

With insights gathered from the previous phase, you're now in a position to create a concise, actionable problem statement that clearly outlines the problem to be solved. This statement acts like a north star that guides the decisions and activities of the team, always keeping them on track and moving in the right direction.

Ideate

It's brainstorming time, where your team gets to come up with a broad range of potential solutions, no matter how outlandish they seem. Create a judgment-free zone where quantity takes precedence over quality and by the end of this activity, you'll have enough ideas to be able to narrow down to a select few, which you'll use to move into the next phase.

Prototype

As this is a highly collaborative process, make sure you're involving and communicating with not only stakeholders but developers too. Developers know exactly what's achievable from a technical standpoint, so use their insight and expertise to help you design realistic and technically feasible products from the get-go.

Your initial design should consist of a low-fidelity, semi-functional prototype, wireframe, or mockup (which will become more refined with each iteration) that demonstrates the core features, functions, and basic interactions of the potential product—just enough to elicit useful feedback from your various audiences, whether internal or external. Think about the top three things a user would want to do, and make sure these are front and center in your design—both easy to find and complete.

Test

You've completed the conceptual design, but how useful and usable is it, and does it meet your users' needs? Usability testing will reduce your risk of building the wrong solution, allowing you to test your prototypes on real or representative users so you can elevate understanding, receive feedback, and catch early design flaws.

"Throwaway" low-fidelity designs encourage early experimentation and speedy iteration—it's much easier to make changes or improvements at this stage in the process than it is later with a more fleshed-out, complete design. Interestingly enough, low-fidelity designs make people feel less intimidated, so suggestions and feedback are more readily provided. Use this knowledge to your advantage.

As this approach is not a linear process, results from this phase will lead to refinements being made to those of previous phases until you're satisfied with the results (or rather your users are) and you have a finalized high-fidelity design that is ready to hand off to developers for preparation and release.

Figure 12: The design thinking process

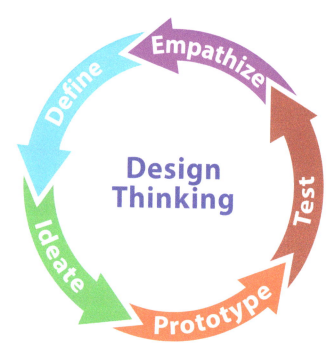

Agile

In today's rapidly changing, customer-driven marketplace, the only way an organization can keep up is to become more "agile" in its processes.

In the 1990s, software development teams were frustrated with rigid, traditional methods (like Waterfall) that lacked flexibility and adaptability. In 2001, a group of visionary developers, who were tired of these antiquated, cumbersome ways, came together and designed a lightweight framework that became known as the Agile Manifesto, which can be found at agilemanifesto.org.

The Agile Manifesto

We are uncovering better ways of developing software by doing it and helping others do it. Through this work we have come to value:

Individuals and interactions over processes and tools
Working software over comprehensive documentation
Customer collaboration over contract negotiation
Responding to change over following a plan

That is, while there is value in the items on the right, we value the items on the left more.

In short, Agile is a flexible, collaborative approach to project management that allows for the incremental, iterative approach to software development. This nimble way of thinking incorporates continuous testing, learning, and a responsiveness to change (whether due to changing requirements, priorities, focus, market trends, or customer needs).

Once a team is made aware of a customer problem, a project is broken up into small deliverable chunks (called user stories) that are prioritized and tackled in a series of short cycles known as sprints. Each sprint can last anywhere from one to four weeks—and at the end of a sprint, the team delivers a small piece of working software.

Agile is a philosophy that is guided by a set of principles and is not a single approach that can be applied to every situation. As a result, it has become the umbrella term used for many types of management frameworks and methodologies, including Scrum and Kanban.

Principles behind the Agile Manifesto

We follow these principles:

Our highest priority is to satisfy the customer through early and continuous delivery of valuable software.

Welcome changing requirements, even late in development. Agile processes harness change for the customer's competitive advantage.

Deliver working software frequently, from a couple of weeks to a couple of months, with a preference to the shorter timescale.

Business people and developers must work together daily throughout the project.

Build projects around motivated individuals. Give them the environment and support they need, and trust them to get the job done.

The most efficient and effective method of conveying information to and within a development team is face-to-face conversation.

Working software is the primary measure of progress.

Agile processes promote sustainable development. The sponsors, developers, and users should be able to maintain a constant pace indefinitely.

Continuous attention to technical excellence and good design enhances agility.

Simplicity—the art of maximizing the amount of work not done— is essential.

The best architectures, requirements, and designs emerge from self-organizing teams.

At regular intervals, the team reflects on how to become more effective, then tunes and adjusts its behavior accordingly.

Design Sprints

The design sprint method emerged as a way of combining the concepts of design thinking and agile into one. A design sprint is an intense five-day process in which user-centered teams employ a slightly modified version of the design thinking process to build and test a prototype in just five days.

Originally created by Jake Knapp of Google Ventures and later published in his book called *Sprint: How to Solve Big Problems and Test New Ideas in Just Five Days*, the methodology is being used by some of the most innovative and competitive companies out there, including Google, Uber, Medium, Slack, Facebook, Twitter, Dropbox, and Airbnb.

It's a low-risk, high-value activity that promises results in days, as opposed to teams having to deal with the constant back-and-forth that can sometimes make a project drag on for weeks, if not months. Although a sprint won't leave you with a completely finalized, shippable product, it is still one of the fastest and cheapest ways to get your prototypes in front of users, validate ideas, and gather insights.

As with just about everything in UX design, it is never a one-size-fits-all situation, so it's important to evaluate whether a design sprint is indeed the right tool for the problem at hand. If a company doesn't know its customers very well or already has a clearly defined set of features, then a design sprint may not be the answer. The process is best used when you have a set of questions or many potential solutions that need to be explored. Here's what you'll need to conduct a design sprint:

- A carefully selected self-managing, cross-functional team of five to seven members that includes a facilitator or sprint master (to keep everyone on track), product manager, UX designer, content designer, UX

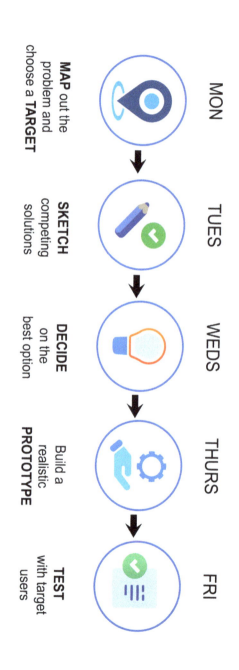

Figure 13: Design sprints methodology

MON — **MAP** out the problem and choose a **TARGET**

TUES — **SKETCH** competing solutions

WEDS — **DECIDE** on the best option

THURS — Build a realistic **PROTOTYPE**

FRI — **TEST** with target users

researcher, developer, and someone from the company's core business department (such as marketing, customer service, or operations).

- The whole week blocked off for the entire team so members are able to work undisturbed (it's important to ensure that all participants are available and present for the duration of a sprint).
- If in person, a dedicated physical location, whiteboards, colored markers, paper, pens, stickers, tape, scissors, and tons of Post-it Notes—and if remote, a digital whiteboard (FigJam, InVision Studio, Mural, or Miro), prototyping tools (Figma, FigJam, Sketch, InVision Studio, or Marvel), and, of course, each participant needs to have a good internet connection and a microphone. Note that remote design sprints will require the facilitator to recruit participants from similar time zones.
- Healthy drinks and snacks like water, tea, coffee, dark chocolate, fruit, nuts, protein bars, and veggies (I know, I know…don't blame me…but it's important to keep those sugar crashes at bay).
- Regularly timed breaks throughout the day.
- No distractions (sorry, folks, that means no cell phones anywhere in sight until break time).

Finally, make no mistake—as fun and exciting as participating in a design sprint can be, there's a lot of hard work involved. Encourage your facilitator to build in a mini celebration that'll function as an official wind-down for the team at the end of the sprint. You'll be so glad you did!

Chapter 5:
A Few Principles of Design

The Grid

A grid is a system of columns and rows that is used to design and organize the layout of a website, app, or digital project with superb precision. It helps create a sense of visual harmony, allowing for congruity across a single site or app even when the content presented within is different or viewed on different platforms, screen sizes, and orientations. Grids also help establish a sense of order and hierarchy that serves to guide the eye, making content easier to identify, scan, or read. Grids are made up of three main elements: columns, gutters, and margins (see figure 14).

Columns: These are the vertical blocks that take up the most real estate. Grid systems can be used to create responsive designs, allowing designers to ensure that layouts look good on a variety of screens. Although the number of columns will vary depending on the medium being designed for, designers typically use up to 12 columns for desktop design, up to eight columns for tablet design, and up to four columns for mobile design.

Gutters: These are the spaces that appear between the columns. They'll be much narrower for mobile than they will be for larger screens.

Margins: These appear as the left and right outermost edges of the grid structure. The size of these margins will increase or decrease in direct proportion to a device's width, and content should never be placed within the area itself.

Figure 14: The grid

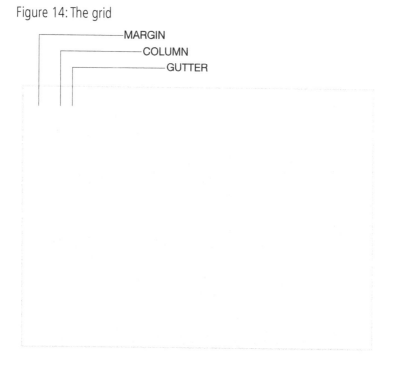

THE MOST COMMON GRID TYPES

The most common types of grids used for website and interface design are column, modular, and hierarchical. A column grid is the most common type and involves dividing a page into vertical columns that design elements can then be aligned to. You can use the grid to establish hierarchy by creating "zones" for different kinds of content. Text or images can occupy a single column or span several, and not all the space has to be filled.

Figure 15: Column grid example (Amazon's account page)

A modular grid consists of intersecting columns and rows that create modules.

Figure 16: Modular grid example (Behance)

Hierarchical grids are used to arrange elements according to importance. These irregular grids use columns, rows, and modules that are completely free-form or composed by combining two or more other grid types. News and media-related sites often use this format, with the most important articles taking up the most space on the grid.

Figure 17: Hierarchical grid example (TNW)

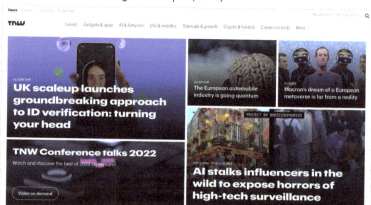

Now that you're aware of grid design, you'll begin to see them everywhere as they serve as the invisible glue behind almost every design or interface you come across. Don't feel confined by the idea of using a grid, however, because now that you know the "rules," it's perfectly OK to intentionally break elements on the grid when you want to create surprise, tension, or a change in rhythm.

Color in Design

It has been said that color (or a selected color palette) accounts for 70 percent of the success of a design—along with the layout (which I hope you'll be using a grid for), text (which we'll learn more about in the next section), and imagery (which, hey, you've just gotta have a good eye for).

Research has shown that different colors, hues, and tones have different psychological effects on the human mind that can dramatically impact behavior and decision-making. This effect will differ according to an individual's preferences, age, gender, and culture.

Red: Symbolizes energy, passion, love, excitement, strength, power, courage, creativity, aggressiveness, anger, and danger

Orange: Symbolizes fun, confidence, motivation, enthusiasm, and success

Yellow: Symbolizes happiness, optimism, positivity, intellect, and creativity

Green: Symbolizes nature, freshness, healing, balance, growth, money, luck, prosperity, vitality, fertility, and envy

Blue: Symbolizes trust, peace, loyalty, reliability, stability, intuition, inspiration, calmness, and competence. Blue may also be associated with sadness and depression (for instance, having the "blues").

Purple: Symbolizes power, royalty, luxury, wealth, wisdom, spirituality, mystery, and magic

Pink: Symbolizes sweetness, friendship, unconditional love, caring, sensitivity, sincerity, and femininity

Gold: Symbolizes understanding and luck

Brown is the color of the earth and symbolizes practicality, trustworthiness, dependability, simplicity, common sense, and "down to earth-ness"

White: Symbolizes truth, purity, cleanliness, clarity, innocence, cleansing, and healing

Black: Symbolizes power, sophistication, reliability, intelligence, confidence, formality, wealth, style, sexiness, and mystery

THE 60-30-10 RULE

Color, just like everything else in life, is best used in moderation. For optimal results, stick to a maximum of three colors within a design, using various shades, tints, or tones for anything additional you may need. The 60-30-10 rule is a tried-and-tested method used by interior designers, but works just as well for UX and brand designers who want to create visually appealing, balanced color schemes.

The rule states that a design's dominant color should take up 60 percent of the available canvas, a complementary secondary color should take up 30 percent of the available canvas, and an accent color should account for approximately 10 percent of the canvas. The dominant and secondary colors should be relatively neutral, with the accent color reserved for "pop" or items you'd like to stand out the most, like a primary call to action button. Use this method to get up and running pretty quickly when you need to create a color palette from scratch.

Quick tip: For a deeper dive into the mechanics of color, google "the color wheel" and "color theory."

COLORS IN ACCESSIBLE DESIGN

Color selection plays a significant role in usability, readability, and the overall user experience. Knowing this, it is imperative that UX and UI designers consider how people with color blindness (also known as color vision deficiency, or CVD) will interact with their website, app, or any other product they may be creating. It goes much deeper than just selecting an aesthetically pleasing palette, as it's estimated that 1 in 12 men (8 percent) and 1 in 200 women (0.5 percent) are affected by some form of color blindness. Worldwide, it is estimated that around 300 million people have color blindness, which, coincidentally, is about the same number as the entire population of the United States.

In one type of color blindness, individuals cannot distinguish between red and green, and in another, they cannot differentiate between blue and yellow. In extremely rare cases, individuals cannot perceive color at all and everything appears to them in various shades of gray. So, now that you know what you know:

- Avoid designs that rely heavily on red and green, blue and yellow, blue and green, yellow and red, or purple and red color schemes.
- Avoid overlaying text on a background with similar color values. Your text-to-background contrast ratio should be at least 4.5 to 1, which can be checked using the WebAIM Contrast Checker Tool found online.
- Limit color schemes to three hues (as already advised) to increase the chance that people with color-deficient vision can distinguish between them.
- Never place similar colors next to each other.
- Never use color alone to convey meaning for things like error states, success states, or system warnings—incorporate messaging or iconography that help to clearly identify exactly what's going on.

- To provide emphasis, always use other visual cues in addition to color–bold or italic text, icons, symbols, glyphs, bullets, or borders.
- When using color to differentiate items in infographics, graphs, or charts, add texture, shapes, or patterns to the color blocks that help to further distinguish items.
- Always underline links that appear within content (and ensure the hand or pointer cursor appears when the link is hovered over).
- Always use distinctly different hues for links and visited links.

Check the Resources section at the back of the book for a comprehensive list of tools for creating balanced color palettes and color accessibility testing solutions.

Typography

According to Wikipedia, typography is the art and technique of arranging type to make written language legible, readable, and appealing when displayed. The arrangement of type involves selecting typefaces, point sizes, line lengths, line-spacing (leading) and letter-spacing (tracking), and adjusting the space between pairs of letters (kerning).

Quick tip: A typeface is a collection of related fonts, such as Arial or Helvetica, and a font refers to a particular variation (weight, width, or style, etc.) within that typeface, for example, Arial bold.

Basically, there are two main classifications of typefaces: serif and sans serif. Serif fonts have small extra strokes attached to the ends of letters (what you're reading right now is a serif font), and sans serif fonts do not ("sans" is Latin for *without*). (See the "Typography" headline and all headings.)

When it comes to print design, studies have shown that serif fonts are easier to read, because the serifs on the letters serve as guidelines for the eye; therefore, serif fonts are recommended for displaying long-form passages of text (better known as body text). Sans serif fonts, on the other hand, have been deemed as tiring on the eyes for large amounts of text and so are recommended to be reserved for headlines, subheads, and sidebar information.

This reasoning was somewhat turned upside down with the introduction of digital interfaces. Due to the low resolution of screens in the early days, serif fonts often appeared blurry depending on the size of the type or the device being used. As a result, sans serif fonts became preferred and were deemed more readable for *both* body and headline text on these low-res devices.

With recent advancements in technology (namely, HD and Retina displays), this is now less of a problem, and both serif and sans serif fonts display easily without issue. However, as the focus shifts to creating more inclusive, equitable designs, this is definitely something you should take into consideration when deciding on the fonts that will make up the majority of your interface.

GUIDELINES FOR SELECTING "USABLE" TYPEFACES

Usable typefaces should be legible, readable, accessible, and scalable. Let's start with a few definitions:

Legible: Legibility refers to how well an individual character can be distinguished from another within a typeface, for instance how easy it is to distinguish between 0 and O, or I, l, and 1 (the number)—particularly when displayed at a smaller size.

Readable: Readability refers to how easy it is for a user to interpret, understand, and digest content that appears in the form of words, sentences, or paragraphs.

Accessible: Accessible typefaces are easy to see, read, and understand by all people (regardless of ability) and do not exclude readers or slow down the reading speed of any user, including those with vision impairments or reading disabilities. To learn more or to ensure compliance, check W3C's Web Content Accessibility Guidelines (WCAG).

Scalable: Scalable typefaces can be reduced or enlarged without distortion, and adapt or readjust according to screen size.

Type tips:
- Although your computer comes with hundreds of preinstalled fonts, you only need two—one for headlines and one for body text. Two fonts are sufficient, because font families contain numerous styles (bold, extra bold, italic, condensed, etc.) that affect the look, shape, and weight of letters, which allows enough room to provide for both consistency and variety.
- Steer away from obscure, flashy, unusual typefaces that can be hard to read. (A list of my recommended, favorite typefaces is coming up next.)
- Don't use similar colors for text and its background. The more visible (and discernible) the text, the faster users are able to scan and read. There are plenty of good contrast-checking tools available online, or you can check W3C's recommendations. I also recommend visiting Contrastrebellion.com if you're interested in finding out more.

- Organize content according to priority—use a font's size, weight, and color to establish a visual hierarchy with headings, subheads, and body text that effectively guide a user through the most important elements on the screen.
- Always use short, simple sentences.
- Use centered text sparingly, if at all.
- Never use all caps for more than one line of text.
- The optimal line length for body text is 50–75 characters for desktop and 30–40 characters for mobile.
- Base font sizes should range between 16 and 26 pixels (px) and never appear smaller than 12px.
- For the spacing between lines (otherwise known as line height or leading), you should start with 1.5 times the selected font size and adjust from there. Lines that are too tight can be hard to scan, and if they're too loose, they appear to be unrelated to each other, which can cause confusion for a reader.
- WCAG recommends that it should be possible for users to zoom in up to 200 percent to make text larger on a website. So once your variables are set, check several devices to ensure that your font scales well up to this value.

RECOMMENDED TYPEFACES

I'm literally just cutting and pasting my go-to list of typefaces that I have stored in my notebook. Although I may not end up there, it is usually a great place for me to start. The list saves me from having to scroll through hundreds of different typefaces, because, well…I'm particular like that.

The more you play with type and notice the subtle nuances, the more you'll see how they all have different personalities in the ways in which they're able to present and convey information. Have fun with it all; combine a serif with a sans serif or put two sans serifs together using the same text for the headline and body, and see if you can "feel" the difference each particular font (or font combination) conveys.

SERIF	SANS SERIF	APP TYPEFACES
Baskerville	Arial	**Abril Fatface**
Bembo	Avant Garde	**Anton**
Bodoni	BEBAS NEUE	**Arimo**
Caslon Pro	Eurostile	Avenir
Century OS	Franklin Gothic	BEBAS NEUE
Didot	**Frutiger**	Futura
Garamond Pro	Futura	**Helvetica Neue**
Goudy OS	Gill Sans	Inter
Janson Text	Helvetica	Lato
Palatino	Inter	Montserrat
Sabon LT Std	Myriad Pro	Nexa
Stone Serif Std	Optima	Open Sans
	Univers	**Oswald**
		Playfair Display
		Raleway
		Roboto
		San Francisco
		Source Sans Pro
		Univers LT Std

Chapter 6:
Design Systems

Although we just looked at a few principles of design, a good design system will do most of the heavy lifting for you. A *system* is defined as a collection of elements or components that are organized for a common purpose. A *design system*, then, is an ever-evolving, reusable collection of the company's preferred components, patterns, and guidelines which serves as the single source of truth for a company's end-to-end design language.

What a Design System Contains

Design systems vary from company to company, depending on the size and maturity of the in-house design practice and the needs of the product team. But at the very least, most will contain the following:

A Style Guide

The rules, standards, and instructions on how a brand's identity should look, act, and sound across mediums such as digital, print, and broadcast. Usage guidelines are provided for colors, fonts, the logo, imagery, illustrations, icons, motion, sound, etc. Some style guides also include brand rules for creating content, focusing on the voice (personality), tone (mood), style, vocabulary, grammar, and various other specifics.

A Component Library

A collection of premade, reusable UI elements (such as buttons, text fields, drop-down lists, tooltips, etc.) that make up the building blocks of a design. The library serves as a one-stop shop for designers and developers alike, as each UI element is presented along with its corresponding snippet of production-ready code (think HTML, CSS, JavaScript, etc.) used by developers to implement designs.

A Pattern Library

These feature collections of UI elements or components that are combined to present recommended solutions to design problems in the form of layouts or templates that typically make up the page of a website or screen of an app.

Accessibility Guidelines

All good design systems will not only have accessibility standards built directly into the design and code of each component but will also provide documentation in the form of guidelines, rules, and recommendations that help teams learn about and create accessible designs that comply with the Web Content Accessibility

Guidelines found at www.w3.org/TR/WCAG20. It is estimated that more than a billion people around the world have some form of disability, so following these guidelines will make content accessible to a wider range of people no matter what their level of physical or cognitive ability.

The Benefits of a Design System

The benefits of a design system include the following:
- Enables standardization—there's a single point of reference for the majority of UX and UI decisions.
- Presents a unified, branded, cohesive, trustworthy experience for customers.
- Leverages best practices. Design systems capture tried-and-tested best practices that can be readily shared across teams.
- Promotes cross-functional collaboration. Having shared names for components, patterns, and conventions increases collaboration, understanding, and alignment within and across product teams.
- Lets new designers and developers onboard quickly and begin working almost right away.
- Promotes efficiency. There's no need to design, code, or even think about the same element twice; simply drag and drop items straight into your designs.
- Allows for the effective use of resources. With basic problems already solved, product teams can focus on solving more complex UX problems and less on the actual UI components or patterns needed to do so.
- Contains built-in accessibility standards.
- Helps mitigate technical and design debt, which happens when there is an overabundance of non-reusable and inconsistent styles being used that are almost impossible to maintain and update over time.

- Helps "future-proof" designs–applying changes to a certain component means all instances of that component are instantly updated across the board, as opposed to having to hunt down and update each individual one.

Chapter 7:
Landing a Job in UX

Your Résumé

Before you can land the job of your dreams in UX, you'll need to create a résumé that can help you do so. The résumé is your first opportunity to show a company just how user-centric your designs can be. Put yourself in the shoes of the hiring manager who wades through hundreds of applications daily—what can *you* do to make their life easier? Create a user-friendly, skimmable document that allows for quick discovery of all the relevant skills, experience, and education you possess.

It will be necessary to thoroughly read and reread the job description to decipher exactly what a company needs. Tweak your résumé to highlight your relevant skills, making sure to incorporate any major keywords that appear in the listing.

As a part of the initial screening process, some companies use an applicant tracking system (ATS), which automatically filters and rejects résumés that do not contain relevant keywords. It's highly unlikely that these will ever make it to a hiring manager's desk, so do what you can to avoid this auto-reject pile.

While most companies accept résumés in a variety of formats, PDF should always be your default choice, as this ensures that formatting remains the same regardless of the device or platform your document is viewed on. The majority of word processors have an "Export to PDF" function, so this should not be a problem.

WHAT TO INCLUDE

Your name and contact information:
- Name
- Email address
- Phone number
- Website address
- A link to your portfolio
- A link to your LinkedIn profile
- A link to your Twitter feed (a recruiter is likely to scour your social media accounts, so get them cleaned up if you feel that it's necessary, prior to submitting your résumé.)
- A link to your blog (if at all related to the position at hand)

Education: List your education history including the school, your major, your GPA (if it's one you're proud of), and any awards you've received for degrees, courses, or certifications—whether complete or in progress.

Skills and Tools: What skills are in demand for UX designers and what exactly is the company looking for? User-centered design, design thinking, UX strategy, information architecture, task flows, user flows, sitemaps, wireframes, prototyping, interaction design, usability testing, etc. How about tools? Figma, Sketch, InVision Studio, Axure RP, Photoshop, etc. Create a bulleted list highlighting everything you've used or, at the very least, are familiar with.

Relevant Experience: It is standard to list your experience in reverse chronological order. Include the employer's name, your title, and dates of employment, along with a short description of your responsibilities, duties, and significant results. Display this information using bulleted lists that contain no more than five bullets per entry. If available, also provide any metrics that helped to quantify your results.

If you're completely new to the field, there's a good chance you have relatable professional experience with transferable skills, whether you were a developer, graphic designer, web designer, architect, or nurse. Just be ready to explain the ways in which your previous role has prepared you for a career in UX.

Those fresh out of college should detail any coursework, assignments, internship work, or passion projects completed, including the steps taken, what was learned, and the results achieved.

A Summary Statement: Although summary statements are declining in popularity, I personally still use one. It gives the chance for a hiring manager to get the gist of who you are and what you're about in a couple of sentences without the need to even scan your résumé. Of course, this tiny storytelling opportunity should be done well and written accurately for maximum effect.

WHAT NOT TO INCLUDE

Typos, misspellings, or grammatical errors:
This is the first thing that'll get your résumé tossed, so
make sure it's free of spelling and grammatical errors.

Broken links: Check that all links are working and
lead to the correct locations.

Formatting errors: Print your résumé and read it
out loud. It's amazing what you'll catch in print versus
what you see on screen. Make sure columns and spacing are neatly aligned and contribute to the overall
legibility of the design.

Multiple pages: Although you may be fortunate
enough to have several pages' worth of experience, a
busy hiring manager just doesn't have the time to read
it all. List what's most recent and relevant, and use your
website or portfolio for any additional information you
may want to provide.

To fit more information on a page, split your doc
into three columns. The first column should list your
contact info, portfolio link, education, skills, and tools;
your experience and summary should span the other
two. You'll find examples of this format, and templates
too, available online.

Too many colors: It's recommended that you stick
to plain old black and white, with the addition of an
accent color for pop, if desired. Ensure that any color
you add is still readable in case your document happens to be printed in black and white.

Novelty fonts: Select no more than two basic, readable fonts (like Arial, Helvetica, or Century Gothic, at a font size between 10 and 12 for body text). Use bold, italics, and capitalization–or simply increase the size of other elements–as needed for emphasis.

Photos: Including a photo as a part of your résumé is considered unprofessional, has the potential to distract from your skills and experience, and can wreak havoc on the ATS system (if a company indeed uses one). My advice is to go ahead (no pun intended) and save that killer headshot for your LinkedIn profile instead.

Your Portfolio

A UX design portfolio is a showcase of your best work. It should contain three or four projects that sufficiently demonstrate your range of UX skills. The most common formats for portfolios are a website, a PDF document (remember what you learned about PDF formatting), or a website that contains a link to a downloadable PDF. Look online for inspiration and to figure out what will work best for you.

Hosting companies such as Squarespace and Wix offer easy-to-use portfolio templates that can get you up and running in no time–no coding skills required. I actually created my portfolio in Figma (Apple Keynote, Microsoft PowerPoint, or Google Slides will work just as well), which I exported to a PDF and host on a WordPress site. If all that sounds like way too much going on, just stick with the simpler options of Squarespace or Wix.

I had originally featured my projects as individual web pages on my website, but I figured it required too much clicking around to navigate and view each one. Linking to my PDF requires one click, and a potential employer has everything they need at their fingertips, literally. Great UX? I'd say so. Also, as far as pacing, I find it much easier to go through my projects slide by slide, as opposed to scrolling through an almost infinite web page–but once again, do what works best for you.

The whole point of your portfolio is to demonstrate your process and give a potential employer a glimpse into how much of your experience is relevant to the challenges you may face at their company. You'll be judged on how well you communicate and convey ideas–another critical UX skill. Make sure to always explain the "why" behind your designs and include any methods you may have used to validate them.

Much like a résumé, your portfolio needs to be skim-mable–make sure all copy is simple, straightforward, and to the point. Although you *want* to explain absolutely everything, there really is no need. The average UX recruiter will spend less than five minutes skimming through, so make every word and asset you include count.

Taking a content-first approach, each project should contain the following information:

- A meaningful headline
- The what (to provide context)
- The problem you were attempting to solve
- The type(s) of research performed
- The market opportunity being taken advantage of (this is optional)
- A list of key team members and their roles
- Your specific role and duties
- Concepts, ideas, and deliverables either used or created during the process. This could be low- to high-fidelity wireframes, prototypes, personas, user journeys, task flows, usability testing results, etc.

- The final outcome or solution, with applicable metrics if available (for instance, increased sign-ups, revenue, etc.)
- Next steps (also optional)

This is your chance to show exactly how you go about solving UX problems, taking into consideration the design thinking process presented in chapter 4 and the ways in which it was weaved into the steps outlined above. Connecting the dots yet?

A typical presentation will last around 45 minutes to an hour, giving you just enough time to go over two to three projects maximum. Those new to the field should, as mentioned, feature any coursework, assignments, internship work, or passion projects, broken out and presented in the format above.

Be sure to make your presentation somewhat of a two-way conversation. If the interviewer does not interrupt or ask questions as you present, be sure to pause, take a breath, and ask if they have any questions for you. Aim to keep them interested and engaged throughout the process. Here are some questions you might receive during the course of your presentation:

- What challenges did you face while working on project X? How did you work through some of those challenges?
- If you had more time to work on project X, what would you change or do differently?
- Was there anyone on the team who was difficult to work with? How did you handle the situation?
- Can you tell me about a time when a project didn't go as planned? What did you learn from it?
- How did you resolve any design problems you were stuck on?

- Describe a situation in which you didn't have enough information to make an informed decision. What did you do?
- What kind of research was performed and at what stage in the process?
- What experience do you have with design systems?
- How do you hand off your designs to development?

10 Typical Interview Questions

Your interviewer will be looking to determine if you're the right person for the position by assessing how you work, think, reason, collaborate, and communicate. Here you'll find some of the most common interview questions you're likely to encounter, whether during the initial phone screening or sometime later in the process.

Some interviews take on a casual tone, while others can feel more formal and sometimes even intense. Either way, practicing your answers in advance will enable you to feel more confident and get prepared for what can be, for some, a nerve-racking experience.

1. Tell me about yourself.

This is a great warm-up question that's typically used to kick the interview process into gear. Here you get to introduce yourself and share a little about your background and your journey into UX. Don't ramble, and don't be too detailed or too personal. Just provide relevant highlights from your experience, training, and education, as well as what excites you most about the field and the role in question.

2. Describe a strength of yours.

Which of your skills, talents, qualities, or experiences do you think the company will benefit from the most? In what ways do *you* think differently? I mean, you could google a set of generic answers to the question, but if all the other applicants are doing the same, then you have no way of truly standing out and being remembered–so just be genuine. Think about projects you've successfully completed and the types of compliments you've received in the past, whether from coworkers, teachers, family, or friends. Try to determine the traits you possess that best fit the job. Once you have a few in mind, be ready to back them up with relevant stories or examples.

3. Describe a weakness of yours.

It may seem counterintuitive to discuss a weakness with a potential employer but nobody's perfect–and how you respond can demonstrate your level of self-awareness and capacity for professional growth. Discuss a weakness or two along with the steps you're taking (or have taken) to overcome them and everything you learned, as a result, along the way.

4. How do you define UX and UX design?

Your interviewer is not interested in a canned, textbook response but wants to hear your personal definition of UX and the ways in which you relate to the field. What's the benefit of UX? Why is it so important to champion the user? And what value does it provide for a business? Your answer should be based on your own personal experience, whether from the perspective of a practitioner or a consumer.

5. What kinds of research methods have you used?

What an interviewer wants to know here is how you validate your designs. Give examples of research methods you've used, the insights you gained, and how they were applied to improving the product or the user experience overall. Were you able to quantify results in some way: increasing clicks, downloads, time-on-page, conversions, etc., or decreasing bounce rates or help desk calls? If possible, make sure to cite metrics that demonstrate how your design positively contributed to a company's bottom line.

6. How would you improve the UX of our product?

Truth be told, this one caught me off guard as a rookie. I'd done everything I needed to prepare for the interview—evidently *other than* figure out how I'd improve the UX of the company's site. Luckily for me, the site was pretty outdated and I was easily able to give recommendations, proceed to the next step, and eventually get the job. *But,* had this book been around then, there'd have been no need for my heart to skip a beat the way it did that day.

Demonstrate a genuine interest in the role by reviewing the company's product, service, website, or app—maybe even taking the time to perform a competitive analysis that will show not only your level of interest but the value you can provide. Lean into what you learned about UX design from chapter 1 and show off some of that knowledge of what constitutes good (and not-so-good) design. Whether you land the job or not, the education you receive from carrying out this exercise alone will be more than worth it in the long run.

7. Where do you find inspiration?

Your answer to this will show your interest in the field and demonstrate that you're a lifelong learner who's always looking for the latest developments and significant design trends–which is exactly what a company needs. Discuss books you've read; blogs, podcasts, or leaders you follow; social media channels you subscribe to; events you attend (virtual or otherwise); and webinars, workshops, or courses you've signed up for. Check the Resources section for ideas on where you can go for (UX) inspiration.

8. Why do you want to work here?

Your answer should focus on how a company's mission, values, purpose, and brand align with your own personal values and goals (which is, hopefully, why you've decided to interview with them in the first place).

What customer pain points are they attempting to address? How long have they been in business? What's the name of the founder or CEO? How many employees do they have? What's listed on the "About Us" page? What kind of topics are featured on their blog? How about their social media? Does an internet search pull any recent articles or news stories about them?

Do your own version of a background check to ensure that the company and role you're applying for will be able to satisfy you over time, as I'm pretty sure you don't want to be going through this interview process again, anytime soon. Check sites like Glassdoor or Blind to uncover any additional information you may need.

9. What are your salary expectations?

I once read the book *Never Split the Difference: Negotiating As If Your Life Depended On It,* by former hostage negotiator Chris Voss and Tahl Raz—and my key takeaway was that you should *never* be the first to throw out a number. Although there are many other factors to take into consideration with regard to your overall compensation (like work-life balance, number of vacation days, the benefits package, possible yearly bonus, stock incentives, allocated training budget, and tuition reimbursement programs, just to name a few), you should have at least done enough research to come up with an appropriate range.

Flip the question back on the employer to see if you can get a number out of them first, or push for a range. My textbook answer is usually something along the lines of "Although salary's important, if we agree that I'm a good fit for the position then I'm sure we can come to a salary that will be mutually agreeable for us both."

Salary negotiation can be the most uncomfortable part of the entire process—that's why it's imperative to know what's going on in the industry. It's just as important to know your worth—the last thing you want to experience is being in a job where you feel like you're being underpaid or being taken advantage of, which will be a huge demotivator in itself.

Negotiate in a way that allows for an agreeable and fair number for all parties involved, and if you have to walk away, that's okay too. Once you get to a certain level and are confident in what you bring to the table, it's important to know (and stick by) your worth.

For salary information, visit sites like Glassdoor or Salary. Robert Half also puts out a yearly salary guide that I've found to be super helpful in the past.

10. What questions do you have for me?

This is typically the last question asked during the interview process, and any candidate worth their salt will have two or three questions (I mean answers) ready to go, so go ahead and ask something. Don't ever feel too intimidated to ask a question. As a UX designer that's all you'll be doing anyway (who, what, where, when, why, and how), so you may as well start now. Your interviewer will not only evaluate how well you communicate but also whether you have the ability to ask good questions. Strategically ask questions that get to the crux of what you really want to know about the company.

In total transparency once again, I'm going to simply cut and paste a few of the questions I tweak or add to, depending on what's most important for me to know about the particular company I'm interviewing with. You should do the same—select or create questions that are most meaningful to you. Oh, and of course, it's perfectly fine to deviate from the script if something arises that piques your interest as you progress through. Here we go:

- What are the top priorities for the business and how does UX fit into that?
- Where is the UX team strongest and weakest?
- What's the greatest challenge the UX team is facing right now?

- What would you say are the most important skills and strengths you'd want to see in the person hired for this position?
- How many people are on the design team?
- How is it arranged as far as integrating and working with other teams?
- What is the relationship between content and design? How do they typically work together?
- Can you describe your onboarding process? How will I get up to speed?
- Are there opportunities for training and progression within the role or the company itself?
- Do both design and content have a seat at the table early in the process?
- How did you go about defining the problem space?
- What would make you consider a project a success?
- With a company that's distributed as this one is, what do you do to encourage team building for your employees?
- How do you mitigate the problem of teams working in silos?
- What do you enjoy the most about working here? What about your job keeps you motivated?

Quick tip: To wrap up answering a question and avoid that awkward silence that can sometimes occur at the end of a reply, finish by referring back to the interviewer's question–for example, "So that's how I'd define UX." You'll thank me later!

The Design Challenge

The design challenge is used by an employer to learn more about an applicant's design process and their approach to problem solving, which will give them insight into how you're likely to approach problems if working for their company.

The challenge may be in the form of a take-home project which will need to be completed within a specified time period, or it may be a live 30- to 60-minute whiteboarding session (whether virtual or in person) where you'll be given a design problem and asked to come up with a solution on the spot.

Members on the interviewing team will take on different roles, from user to stakeholder to product manager, etc., and it's your duty to probe each one for context, scope, and insights (it *is* supposed to be a collaborative process) as you talk through the reasoning behind your design decisions, which you'll be illustrating on the whiteboard the entire time. During the exercise, members on the interview team will be looking to answer questions like:

- Is the designer comfortable thinking visually and drawing ideas on the fly?
- How collaborative are they?
- Did they make accurate assumptions and ask the right kinds of questions?
- Did they respond well to feedback and constructive criticism?
- Will they make a great addition to the team?
- How well did they communicate?
- How well did they manage the time?
- Did they demonstrate user-centric design, applying design thinking principles as a part of the process?
- Did they focus wholly on the UI, jumping straight into a solution without fully understanding the user or the problem first?
- Are they familiar with basic design principles and patterns?
- Did they write down a list of tasks, features, or goals for the exercise?

- Did they take any existing mental models into consideration?
- Did they mention any limitations or constraints?
- Did they give suggestions on what they would like to uncover from user research?
- Did they notice any weaknesses in the solution and suggest improvements themselves?
- Did they talk about alternatives or other use cases? How about any edge cases?
- Did they take any other factors, such as accessibility, into consideration?
- Did they suggest more ideas and features outside of the immediate scope of the exercise?

Use your time wisely and remember to keep an eye on the clock the entire time. One of my favorite quotes from Einstein is, "If I had an hour to solve a problem, I'd spend 55 minutes thinking about the problem and five minutes thinking about solutions." Loosely take that kind of thinking into the exercise, remembering that the interviewer is not looking for a near-pixel-perfect design but is more focused on your thought process in getting there.

Quick tip 1: Find design challenge generators at Designercize (designercize.com) and Sharpen (sharpen.design).

Quick tip 2: See the appendix on the following page for ideas around the type of thinking that goes into solving a design challenge. As a basis, I typically like to solution around: who, what, when, where, why, and how.

Appendix:
Kiosk Design Exercise

Taken from chapter 3's Task Analysis section, this will serve to add a little more context around the problem as you work toward generating a solution.

Challenge:
Design a self-serve, kiosk-style liquid soap and shampoo dispenser

Who is the user?
Female, 28, married, USA, college graduate, intermediate tech level

What is the problem, need, or motivation?
- User wants to cut costs on soap and shampoo for her growing family
- She cares about the planet and is concerned about waste
- She wants to refill liquid soap or shampoo at the nearest self-service dispensary kiosk
- She needs to refill conveniently, preferably on her grocery store run

How will the user know when the task is complete?

When she has a quick, easy, cost-effective way to refill liquid soap and shampoo

What problem is the business having?

- The increase in cost of plastic containers
- Passing the plastic container cost down to the customer's which makes the product more expensive
- Wants to be more eco-friendly

How will the business know if the product (or feature) is a success? What are some of the key performance indicators (KPIs)?

- Business meets projected sales
- Business is able to pass cost savings down to customers (wants to target budget-conscious shoppers)
- Manages to retain repeat, loyal customers
- Customers positively share their experience online and raise awareness of the service

Where and when does the problem present itself for the user? What triggers the action?

The problem occurs at home when the user runs out of soap or shampoo

Where will the product or service be used?

At the local grocery store

What are you designing for? (Website, mobile app, watch, desktop, kiosk, etc.)

Kiosk

What are the assumptions? What will users be expected to know, do, be, or have to start the task?

- The empty container fits within the size constraints of the kiosk
- User has downloaded and registered in-app
- User has an electronic form of payment (if not preregistered in-app)

What are some constraints?

- The kiosk only carries specific brands
- No cash payments are accepted
- There is a minimum and maximum container size requirement

The steps: (from chapter 3's Task Analysis section)

1. User downloads and registers in-app
2. User searches in app for nearest refill station
3. User drives to nearest refill station
4. User scans QR code from app
5. User confirms payment method to use
6. Slot opens and user puts appropriately sized container in slot (sensor automatically detects container size)
7. User selects "Soap" or "Shampoo"
8. User selects the desired brand from the list
9. Cost savings are displayed on-screen and user accepts the dollar amount charge for the transaction
10. Liquid is dispensed
11. Kiosk asks: "Fill Another?"
12. User selects "No"
13. Payment is charged, user receives text receipt, and transaction details are registered to the app

With a good grasp of the user and the problem, the desired goals (for both the business and the user), and the tasks outlined, you're now in a position to start designing the screens that will make up the solution to this problem.

Resources

All links to the following resources can be found on uxtogo.net. Enjoy!

Recommended Reads

Articulating Design Decisions: Communicate with Stakeholders, Keep Your Sanity, and Deliver the Best User Experience (2nd Edition)
by Tom Greever

Cracking Information Architecture: The Definitive Field Guide for Designers, Business Managers and Project Teams
by Colin Shanley

Design for How People Think: Using Brain Science to Build Better Products
by John Whalen

The Design of Everyday Things
by Don Norman

Designing with the Mind in Mind: Simple Guide to Understanding User Interface Design Guidelines
by Jeff Johnson

Designing Interfaces: Patterns for Effective Interaction Design (3rd Edition)
by Jenifer Tidwell, Charles Brewer, and Aynne Valenci

Dieter Rams: Ten Principles for Good Design
by Cees W. De Jong, Klaus Klemp, Jorrit Maan, and Erik Mattie

Don't Make Me Think, Revisited: A Common Sense Approach to Web Usability (3rd Edition)
by Steve Krug

The Elements of User Experience: User-Centered Design for the Web and Beyond (2nd Edition)
by Jesse James Garrett

Evil by Design: Interaction Design to Lead Us into Temptation
by Chris Nodder

Hooked: How to Build Habit-Forming Products
by Nir Eyal

Information Architecture: For the Web and Beyond (4th Edition)
by Louis Rosenfeld, Peter Morville, and Jorge Arango

The Inmates Are Running the Asylum: Why High-Tech Products Drive Us Crazy and How to Restore the Sanity
by Alan Cooper

Keep Going: 10 Ways to Stay Creative in Good Times and Bad
by Austin Kleon

The Laws of Simplicity (Design, Technology, Business, Life)
by John Maeda

The Lean Startup: How Today's Entrepreneurs Use Continuous Innovation to Create Radically Successful Businesses
by Eric Ries

Lean UX: Designing Great Products with Agile Teams (3rd Edition)
by Jeff Gothelf and Josh Seiden

Laws of UX: Using Psychology to Design Better Products and Services
by Jon Yablonski

Microcopy: The Complete Guide (2nd Edition)
by Kinneret Yifrah

The Non-Designer's Design Book (4th Edition)
by Robin Williams

Simple and Usable: Web, Mobile, and Interaction Design (2nd Edition)
by Giles Colborne

Solving Product Design Exercises: Questions & Answers
by Artiom Dashinsky

Steal Like an Artist: 10 Things Nobody Told You About Being Creative
by Austin Kleon

Storytelling in Design: Defining, Designing, and Selling Multidevice Products
by Anna Dahlström

Universal Principles of Design, Revised and Updated: 125 Ways to Enhance Usability, Influence Perception, Increase Appeal, Make Better Design Decisions, and Teach Through Design (2nd Edition)
by William Lidwell, Kritina Holden, and Jill Butler

User Friendly: How the Hidden Rules of Design Are Changing the Way We Live, Work, and Play
by Cliff Kuang

UX Strategy: Product Strategy Techniques for Devising Innovative Digital Solutions (2nd Edition)
by Jaime Levy

UX Blogs

Career Foundry UX Design Blog
careerfoundry.com/en/blog/ux-design

Case Study Club
casestudy.club

Design Lab
designlab.com/blog

Google Design
medium.com/google-design

Inside Design (InVision)
invisionapp.com/inside-design

Mockplus Blog
mockplus.com/blog

Muzli Magazine
medium.muz.li

Nielsen Norman Group
nngroup.com/articles

Smashing Magazine
smashingmagazine.com/category/user-experience

Studio by UXPin
uxpin.com/studio/blog/

Thinking Design by Adobe XD
medium.com/thinking-design

Tubik Blog
blog.tubikstudio.com

Usability Geek
usabilitygeek.com

The UX Blog
medium.theuxblog.com

UX Booth
uxbooth.com

UX Collective
uxdesign.cc

UX Design World
uxdworld.com

UX Hints
uxhints.com

UX Mastery
uxmastery.com

UX Matters
uxmatters.com

UX Myths
uxmyths.com

UX Planet
uxplanet.org

UX Writing Hub
uxwritinghub.com/blog

UX/UI Design Patterns

Collect UI
collectui.com

GoodUI
goodui.org

Page Flows (highly recommended)
pageflows.com

Screenlane
screenlane.com

UI Garage
uigarage.net

UserOnboard
useronboard.com

UXArchive
uxarchive.com

Color Tools and Accessibility Checkers

Color Tools

Canva's image to color palette generator
canva.com/colors/color-palette-generator

Color Hunt's hand-picked palettes
colorhunt.co

ColorSpace's color palette generator
mycolor.space

Colorwise
colorwise.io

Coolors color palette generator
coolors.co

CSS Drive's image to color palette generator
cssdrive.com/imagepalette

Eva Design System
colors.eva.design

Hihayk's color scale generator
hihayk.github.io/scale

Paletton's color scheme designer
paletton.com

PALX's automatic UI color palette generator
palx.jxnblk.com

Accessibility Checkers

Polypanes color contrast checker analyzes and suggests colors that meet the required contrast ratio.
polypane.app/color-contrast

Sim Daltonism for Mac can be used to simulate different types of colorblindness.
michelf.ca/projects/mac/sim-daltonism

Stark's suite of integrated accessibility tools (Works with Figma, Sketch, Adobe XD, and Chrome)
getstark.co

Toptal's color filter lets you test a website to learn how people with different types of color blindness will see your pages.
toptal.com/designers/colorfilter

WAVE's web accessibility evaluation tool
wave.webaim.org

Popular Design Systems

Atlassian Design (Atlassian)
atlassian.design

Carbon Design System (IBM)
carbondesignsystem.com

The QuickBooks Design System (Intuit)
designsystem.quickbooks.com

iOS Human Interface Guidelines (Apple)
developer.apple.com/design/human-interface-guidelines/
platforms/overview

Lightning Design System (Salesforce)
lightningdesignsystem.com

Material Design 3 (Google)
m3.material.io

Polaris (Shopify)
polaris.shopify.com

Design Awards and Inspiration

Awwwards: The awards for design, creativity, and innovation on the internet
awwwards.com

Behance
behance.net

Cover Junkie
coverjunkie.com

Dribbble
dribbble.com

Fast Company's Innovation by Design Awards
fastcompany.com/apply/innovation-by-design

Graphis
graphis.com

Growth Design Case Studies
growth.design/case-studies

Siteinspire
siteinspire.com

The Webby Awards
webbyawards.com

Yanko Design
yankodesign.com

Glossary

A/B testing: Method of testing in which two different designs are compared against each other to determine which is preferred or performs the best

Accessible design: The concept of whether a service or product can be used by the broadest range of individuals, irrespective of ability

Adaptive: An interface that's designed and built to automatically adapt to various screen sizes, orientations, or devices

Agile software development: A flexible, collaborative approach to project management that allows for the incremental, iterative approach to software development

Alternative text: Short text description of an image on a website inserted as an HTML attribute

Animation: A simulation of movement by inanimate objects

Annotation: Explanation or comment used to communicate behavior or functionality on a wireframe or prototype

Augmented reality (AR): An interactive experience where digital information is integrated with a user's environment in real time

Back-end developer: Builds and maintains the behind-the-scenes technology that occurs when performing an action on a website that the user does not visibly see, like the storage of login IDs and passwords or the capturing of information submitted though a contact form

Backlog: A prioritized list of tasks (or features) to be implemented as part of a software product or project

Breadcrumb: Secondary navigational aid that shows website users where they are in the website hierarchy (and the path of how they got there)

Call to action (CTA): An interactive UI element on a website or app that prompts a user to take a specific action; for instance, "Sign Up" or "Buy Now"

Card sort: A popular research method in which information is organized, categorized, and labeled based on the feedback received from a selected audience [See closed card sort, hybrid card sort, and open card sort]

Chatbot: A software application used to conduct an online chat conversation via text or speech-to-text that can reply to questions, take instructions, and solve customer support problems without the need for a live human representative

Closed card sort: A research method in which information is organized, categorized, and labeled based on the feedback received from a selected audience and where participants are asked to place items into predefined categories [See card sort, hybrid card sort, and open card sort]

Cognitive load: The amount of mental effort a user has to invest when interacting with a product

Competitive analysis: Identifying and evaluating the relative strengths and weaknesses of a competitor's products or services

Content designer: Plans, writes, edits, and manages content that is informed by research and an understanding of the holistic user journey, to help in the design of websites, apps, and other digital products

Content strategist: Takes a high-level, strategic approach to planning, creating, publishing, and managing content to achieve a specific business or user goal

Content style guide: A company-wide document that outlines a particular brand's rules for creating content; can include decisions about vocabulary, spelling, syntax, grammar, and various other deliberate language choices

Contextual inquiry: Research method in which users are observed in their natural environment in order to understand their tasks and challenges

Conversion rate: The percentage of visitors that complete a targeted transaction online

Copy: The written material of a design

Copy doc(ument): A document that summarizes all copy featured on a website, app, or other digital product

Cross-platform: Software that is designed to work on multiple platforms or operating systems

Customer journey map: A map that visualizes the linear path a customer takes to engage with a particular product or service being offered by a business

Dark patterns: Tricks used in websites and apps that cause a user to unintentionally perform an undesired action, such as unknowingly subscribe to a newsletter

Design debt: The accumulation of design-related inconsistencies in a product over time

Design pattern: A collection of UI elements or components that are combined to present recommended solutions to design problems in the form of layouts or templates that typically make up the page of a website or the screen of an app

Design sprint: Popularized by Google Ventures (GV), an intense five-day process where user-centered teams use a slightly modified version of the design thinking process to build and test a prototype in just five days

Design system: An ever-evolving, reusable collection of the components, patterns, and guidelines that serves as the single source of truth for a company's end-to-end design language

Design thinking: An iterative, nonlinear, user-centric approach to the practical resolution of customer problems

Diary study: Research method that involves providing participants with the materials and structure to record and describe daily events, tasks, and perceptions around a given subject in order to gain insight into their behaviors, activities, and experiences over time

Edge case: An atypical, unusual, or rare circumstance that falls outside the "normal" range or boundaries of a product or service; e.g., a user (or bot) that attempts to log in 10 times in a row in a short period of time

Empathy: The ability to put aside one's own biases and relate to and understand the thoughts, feelings, and experiences of others

End user(s): The set of users that a product or service is intended to serve

Equitable design: Design that takes into account the needs of people from diverse backgrounds who have traditionally been underrepresented, along the lines race, gender, class, religion, sexual identity, sexual orientation, and nationality

Error message: The alert or message presented to a user when something goes wrong

Error rate: Error frequency over a certain period of time

Error recovery: The ability for a user to course-correct and continue to complete a task or goal after some type of error is encountered

Ethnographic field study: A qualitative research method of observing users in their natural environment over a period of time to understand their activities and behaviors

Eye tracking software: Software that uses invisible near-infrared light and high-definition cameras to project light onto the eye to record and measure where a person looks, what they look at, and for how long

Facilitator: A person who moderates a discussion or activity to collect feedback and information

Feature bloat: When a product is overloaded with features and functions and no longer serves core user needs

Fidelity: The level of detail presented in a prototype, mockup, or wireframe–can be low (displays a very rough approximation of the design), medium (displays a little more detail than low fidelity), or high (close in nature to the final design) [See high-fidelity prototype and low-fidelity prototype]

Findable: A measure of how quickly and easily information can be navigated through or found

First click testing: A testing method to see where a user clicks first on a website or app when trying to complete a specific task or goal

Fluid layout: A design technique that automatically scales the layout to fit a browser window or monitor resolution

Focus group: A research method where researchers bring together a small group of people to take part in an interactive discussion about a specific topic (or set of topics) in a moderated environment

Fold: A term that goes back to the days before digital design when newspapers were sold from sidewalk kiosks and the most important, headline-grabbing stories were placed at the top of the page (above the fold) in an attempt to get the immediate attention of passersby; the term is now used in website design to describe the content that is visible to a user when a web page first loads (without the need to scroll)

Font: A particular typeface's weight, width, or style, etc., for example, Arial bold

Font color: The color of the text

Font readability: How easy it is for a reader to interpret, understand, and digest content that appears in the form of words, sentences, or paragraphs in a specific type style

Form elements: Input controls like text fields, checkboxes, radio buttons, submit buttons, and text area

Friction: Anything that makes a task harder and slows down or prevents a user from accomplishing a desired action or task on a website or app

Front-end developer: Uses HTML, CSS, and JavaScript to build the front-end portion of a website that a user sees and interacts with

Gap analysis: A process of comparing the current state with the desired state of an organization

Global navigation: The persistent, unchanging menu that appears on every page of a website that allows a user to easily switch between the top-level pages (or subcategories) presented

Grid system: A system of columns and rows used to design and organize the layout of a website, app, or print project with superb precision

Gutter: The space between columns on a grid system

Happy path: A system's most efficient and effective way to accomplish a task

Heat map: A data visualization that shows how website users click, scroll, or move their mouse on a web page

Heuristic evaluation: An evaluation method used to test the usability of a website or app based on a set of principles which become the "heuristics" of the test; the most widely-known and popularly-used in UX are the "10 usability heuristics" proposed by Jakob Nielsen

Hierarchy: Where elements are organized and presented according to priority or importance

High-fidelity prototype: An interactive prototype that looks very much like the finished product, displaying most of the intended functionality and including the actual content, typography, colors, and other branding elements to be incorporated into the final design [See low-fidelity prototype]

Hybrid card sort: Research method where participants are asked to sort cards into predefined categories (similar to a closed card sort) but are also free to create their own categories outside of what's been provided [See card sort, closed card sort, and open card sort]

Inclusive design: Designing services or products to be accessible to, and usable by, as many individuals and groups as possible, irrespective of background, situation, or ability

Information architect (IA): Professional who increases the usability of a product by structuring, organizing, and labeling content in a clear and logical manner so that information is easy to find, discover, navigate, scan, or read

Information architecture: The structural design of information with the goal of making it easy to find, discover, navigate, scan, or read

Interaction design (IxD): A discipline that specifically focuses on creating engaging interfaces that aid in user interaction with a product or app

Interactive prototype: A simulation of the final product, website, or app that includes basic interactions, transitions, and events that can be used to demonstrate functionality to stakeholders, tease feedback from team members, and help validate concepts with target users

Interface: The means (software or hardware) by which an interaction or communication is achieved with a device

Internationalization (i18n): The practice of designing and developing a product so it can be adapted for users of different cultures, languages, or religions (i18n stands for the number of letters that appear between "i" and "n" in the word *internationalization*)

Interview: A qualitative research method that involves asking open-ended questions to better understand and explore research subjects' opinions, behavior, and experiences

Jargon: Unfamiliar, specialized words or expressions used within a particular profession or group

JavaScript: A programming language used to make web pages interactive

Kerning: The space between the characters in a font

Key performance indicator (KPI): A quantifiable measure of performance over time for a specific business or project goal or objective

Keyword: Words and phrases that people typically type into search engines to find what they're looking for

Labels: The names used for buttons and site navigation, etc.

Landing page: Technically any web page a user lands on in a site, but in the marketing realm, the term is used to describe a stand-alone page that has specifically been created for a marketing or ad campaign

Leading: The vertical space that appears between lines of text. Increasing or decreasing this value can improve or reduce readability.

Learnability: How easy or difficult it is to learn to effectively use a system, interface, or device

Legibility: How well an individual character can be distinguished from another within a particular typeface

Likert scale: A widely used approach to scaling responses in survey research; for instance, a five-point Likert scale that measures the level of confidence in selections can have values that range from "Not confident at all" to "Very confident"

Liquid design: A design technique that automatically scales a page to fit a browser window or monitor resolution

Localization (l10n): Personalizing a national or international product for a local market. Applies to more than just translation—can include changes to idioms, dates and times, currencies, and other aspects of the user experience (l10n stands for the number of letters that appear between "l" and "n" in the word *localization*)

Low-fidelity prototype: A simple sketch or diagram made for gauging feedback on initial concepts that contains lines and boxes to indicate where elements, content, or features will go—with little or no attention paid to the visual design [See high-fidelity prototype]

Mental model: Ways in which one understands the world

Metadata: The pieces of information used to describe various aspects of a digital asset so that asset can be identified and found

Microcopy / UX writing: The clear, concise, sometimes conversational interface copy that helps a user understand, use, and navigate a product

Minimum viable product (MVP): A product launched with only the most important features to an early set of users to provide valuable feedback before developers fully commit more time and resources to features that users may not care about, want, need, or use

Mockup: A realistic visual model of what a final web page or app will look like

Modal: A dialog box that appears on top of the main content when an item is clicked or tapped and requires some type of user action to dismiss

Moderated usability testing: Usability testing with a person to help facilitate or moderate the test

Monochrome: Paintings, drawings, design, or photographs displayed in black and white, in a single color or hue, or in varying tones of a single color

Mood board (also known as an inspiration board): A visual presentation or collage of images, typography, textures, color palettes, and descriptions arranged around a particular subject or theme

Multivariate testing: The testing of three or more options to determine which combination of variations performs the best out of all possible combinations; can be especially useful when you want to test the impact of radical (or many) changes to a web page as opposed to testing the impact of one specific element [See A/B testing]

Navigation: The means by which a user moves between the pages or screens of a website or app

Negative space: Unused space (also known as white space) [See white space]

Nomenclature: The system of naming or classifying things

Observation: Watching how users interact with a product or service in a controlled or natural environment

Omnichannel user experience: The experience a user has completing a single activity while moving across various channels (e.g., phone, website, and a physical location)

Onboarding: The series of steps (or guidance) a new user takes before using a product or service to increase the likelihood of the successful adoption of that product or service

Open card sort: A research method where participants group cards into categories they name and label themselves [See card sort, closed card sort, and hybrid card sort]

Pagination: The process of dividing information into separate distinct pages which are numbered and linked

Pain point: Any UX issue that frustrates a user, slow them down or blocks them from completing a desired task, action, or goal

Paper prototype: A "throwaway" paper representation of a digital product that allows teams to quickly visualize, get feedback, and test initial concepts and ideas

Patterns: Best-practice solutions for how a user achieves a goal. Features collections of UI elements or components that are combined to present recommended solutions to design problems in the form of layouts or templates that typically make up the page of a website or screen of an app.

Persona: A fictional character (composed from the results of qualitative and quantitative user research) that is used to classify and summarize the main characteristics of the most important users a product will serve

Personalization: Tailoring content and functionality to the needs and preferences of an individual user based on specific information about them and their current context

Platform: The hardware or operating system on which a user experiences a product

Plugin: A software module that adds a specific feature, function, or service to a larger system

Pop-up: A window that is automatically invoked when a user loads a web page or performs a specific action

Problem statement: Defines the specific challenge or pain point to be addressed by a company or organization

Product backlog: In agile project management, this refers to a prioritized list of features, functions, updates, bug fixes, infrastructure changes, or other activities to be delivered over time

Product design: The process of creating useful, usable products and experiences by identifying a market opportunity, clearly defining a problem, developing a solution, and validating that solution with users

Product designer: Crafts simple, intuitive, engaging experiences that enable users to easily accomplish their tasks and goals [See user experience design]

Product manager: Responsible for the strategy, planning, forecasting, and development of a feature, product, or service

Progressive disclosure: A method wherein the functionality presented in a user interface progresses naturally from simple to complex in a step-by-step way so as not to frustrate or overwhelm a user with too much information unless they actively choose to seek it out

Prototype: A preliminary design of a product used to test and gather feedback [See high-fidelity prototype and low-fidelity prototype]

Push notification: A message, notification, or call to action that is sent directly to a mobile device

Qualitative research: The study of human behavior that emphasizes nonnumerical insights, focusing on thoughts, feelings, emotions, opinions, and experiences

—answering the "what," "how," and "why" of a user's behavior rather than "how many" or "how much" [See quantitative research]

Quality assurance (QA): The systematic process of determining whether a product or service meets specified requirements and functions free of any defects or bugs; QA specialists intentionally aim to find breaking points in software and products so that users don't have to

Quantitative research: The study of human behavior that focuses on behaviors that can be measured and expressed in numbers or figures [See qualitative research]

Questionnaire (or survey): Qualitative or quantitative research method (depending on the format of questions) used to collect data from individuals about certain topics or experiences

Rapid prototyping: The process of iteratively generating mockups for validating with users or stakeholders

Readability: How easy it is for a user to interpret, understand, and digest content that appears in the form of words, sentences, or paragraphs

Responsive web design (RWD): A practice of crafting websites to provide an optimal viewing experience regardless of platform, screen size, or device

Return on investment (ROI): An approximate measure of an investment's profitability; can be used to help product teams determine whether certain efforts are worth pursuing or assess whether a past effort was worth it

Sans serif: A category of typefaces that do not have small lines attached to the ends of the characters ("sans" means *without*) [See serif]

Scannability: The ease with which a body of text can be read and understood

Screen reader: The interface or software program that allows a blind or visually impaired individual to read text displayed on a computer that has a speech synthesizer or braille display

Screeners: Questions used to narrowly target an audience by qualifying or disqualifying respondents (from taking a survey) depending on how they answer

Search engine optimization (SEO): Techniques to improve a website's ranking in search engine results

Serif: A category of typefaces that have small lines attached to the ends of the characters [See sans serif]

Sitemap: A visual tool for planning and organizing the navigational structure, content, and labeling for the major categories and subcategories of a website or app

Software as a Service (SAAS): A software distribution model in which an app is licensed on a free or subscription basis and hosted remotely over the internet (in the cloud) instead of locally on a machine

Storyboard: A cartoon-like illustration that explains a user problem–depicting the situation that sets it in motion, the thoughts and feelings a user experiences along the way, and the series of actions taken to get the issue resolved

Style guide: The rules, standards, and instructions for how a brand's identity should look, act, and sound across mediums such as digital, print, and broadcast

Survey (or questionnaire): Qualitative or quantitative research method (depending on the format of questions) used to collect data from individuals about certain topics or experiences

Target audience: The intended audience for a product, service, website, or app

Task analysis: A method used to identify and understand the sequence of steps a user must take to accomplish a task or a goal

Task flow: A diagram that depicts the sequence of steps a user must take to achieve a goal

Taxonomy: The way in which information or concepts are grouped, organized, and classified

Technical writer: A professional who transforms complex, technical information into clear, concise, easy-to-understand documentation

Think-aloud method: The process by which a test subject narrates their testing experience as they go, discussing not only what they're doing but why they're doing it

Toast: An informative feedback message on a website or app that provides information regarding the success or failure of an action before automatically disappearing

Tooltip: A small box of information that appears or pops up when a user taps or mouses over a designated graphical element or text

Touchpoint: A particular digital or physical interaction that takes place between a user and an organization

Typeface: A collection of related fonts, for example, Arial or Helvetica

Typography: The art of arranging type to make written material legible, readable, and appealing when displayed

Usability: The extent to which a product is easy, intuitive, efficient, and enjoyable for a customer to use in achieving a task or goal

Usability testing: Techniques used for measuring usability [See usability]

User experience (UX): Everything that happens to a user while using a product or service—including the emotions, attitudes, feelings, reactions, and behaviors that take place during the experience

User experience design (UXD): The practice of crafting simple, intuitive, engaging experiences that enable users to easily accomplish their tasks and goals [See product designer]

User flow: A visual representation of the path a user can take through a system to achieve a specific goal

User interface (UI), or graphical user interface (GUI): The medium through which a user interacts with a product, experience, or device

User interface design: The design of the look, feel, and behavior of an application's interface

User interview: Qualitative research method that involves conducting one-on-one discussions with a participant on a particular topic [See qualitative research and quantitative research]

User journey: The path(s) a user can take to complete a task or achieve a goal

User story: A method in the agile software development process that is used for capturing user requirements (not system requirements) in a short, simple, nontechnical way

User-centered design: An approach to designing a product or service in which focus is placed on users and their needs at every stage of the design process

UX portfolio: A showcase of a designer's best work that demonstrate their design process, problem-solving abilities, and a range of other UX skills

UX researcher: Uses qualitative and quantitative methods to provide insights into user wants, goals, needs, motivations, attitudes, expectations, and pain points so an organization can move from opinion-driven design to a more informed, empathetic, customer-focused, and data-driven design [See qualitative research and quantitative research]

UX writer: They create the clear, concise, sometimes conversational interface copy (microcopy) that helps a user understand, use, and navigate a product

Virtual reality (VR): An immersive, simulated 3D environment that users interact with using special electronics like VR helmets, goggles, gloves, and sensors

Visual design: The use of fonts, colors, images, and other elements to enhance a design or interaction

Visual hierarchy: Where elements are organized according to importance or priority

Voice user interface (VUI): Interface that enables users to interact with systems and devices using voice or speech commands. Siri, Google Assistant, and Alexa are all examples of VUIs

Wayfinding: How a user orients themself through a website, app, or other digital product

Web analytics: Measures, collects, analyzes, and reports user behavior on a website

Web Content Accessibility Guidelines (WCAG): WCAG are focused on providing international technical standards for web content. There are 12 guidelines that are organized under four principles: perceivable, operable, understandable, and robust. The guidelines each have testable success criteria, which are at three levels: A, AA, and AAA.

White space: The blank space that appears between graphics, columns, images, text, or other objects; when used effectively, white space increases legibility and readability [See negative space]

Widget: A small application, or a component of an interface, that displays information or enables a user to perform a function or access a service

Wireframe: A skeletal layout created for testing and feedback purposes that is stripped of visual design but acts as blueprint for a website or application—can range in fidelity from low to high [See high-fidelity prototype and low-fidelity prototype]

About the Author

Lorraine Phillips is a multi-disciplined UX professional with over a decade's worth of experience working with and consulting for digital agencies, startups, small businesses, and Fortune 500 companies. She holds an MBA in business administration, a BS in computer science, and an AA in graphic design. In her free time Lorraine enjoys mentoring and coaching others—as she puts it in her own words, "It's exactly what I was born to do!"

Index

D